A Nature Walk in the City

Louise and Richard Spilsbury

Raintree is an imprint of Capstone Global Library Limited, a company incorporated in England and Wales having its registered office at 7 Pilgrim Street, London, EC4V 6LB – Registered company number: 6695582

www.raintreepublishers.co.uk
myorders@raintreepublishers.co.uk

Edited by Joanna Issa, Penny West, Krissy Mohn, and Gina Kammer
Designed by Cynthia Akiyoshi
Picture research by Elizabeth Alexander and Tracy Cummins
Production by Helen McCreath
Originated by Capstone Global Library Ltd
Printed and bound in China by Leo Paper Group

ISBN 978 1 406 28217 7 (hardback)
18 17 16 15 14
10 9 8 7 6 5 4 3 2 1

ISBN 978 1 406 28222 1 (paperback)
19 18 17 16 15
10 9 8 7 6 5 4 3 2 1

British Library Cataloguing in Publication Data
A full catalogue record for this book is available from the British Library.

Acknowledgements
We would like to thank the following for permission to reproduce photographs:

Alamy: © Julia Gavin, 18, © sandy young, 20, © Washington Imaging, 6; Getty Images: Ditto, front cover; iStock: © txe, 15, back cover; naturepl.com: Laurent Geslin, 14, Meul/ARCO, 17, Nick Upton/2020VISION, 13, Terry Whittaker/2020VISION, 19, 21; Shutterstock: ajt, design element (slug), Alex Staroseltsev, design element (ladybug), Eric Isselee, design element (fox), Evgeniy Ayupov, design element (ant), evronphoto, 5, Iain McGillivray, 9, James Laurie, 16, landysh, 10, Martin Horsky, design element (stone pavement), Mary Rice, design element (bricks), mycteria, design element (cobblestone), Nadiia Korol, 22 top left, oBatchenko, front cover, back cover, Oleksiy Mark, 22 bottom left, Pakhnyushcha, design element (rat), PHOTO FUN, 12 inset, Quang Ho, design element (flower), romrf, 22 bottom right, Sergii Figurnyi, 4, T Cassidy, 22 top right, Tomatito, 11, Valerie Potapova, 8, Voyagerix, 7, back cover left, zebra0209, 12, zhangyang13576997233, design element (leaf).

We would like to thank Michael Bright for his assistance in the preparation of this book.

Every effort has been made to contact copyright holders of material reproduced in this book. Any omissions will be rectified in subsequent printings if notice is given to the publisher.

All the Internet addresses (URLs) given in this book were valid at the time of going to press. However, due to the dynamic nature of the Internet, some addresses may have changed, or sites may have changed or ceased to exist since publication. While the author and publisher regret any inconvenience this may cause readers, no responsibility for any such changes can be accepted by either the author or the publisher.

Contents

Where are we going? 4

What is up on the roof? 6

What grows on the street? 8

What lives in parks? 10

What lives on walls? 12

Is the pavement empty? 14

What lives in the bushes? 16

What animals come out at night? 18

How can I protect city animals? 20

Exploring nature 22

Glossary 23

Find out more 24

Index 24

Some words are shown in bold, **like this**. You can find out what they mean by looking in the glossary.

Where are we going?

We are going for a nature walk in the city. There are lots of plants and animals in a city if you know where to look.

When you walk in a city, watch out for traffic. Do not walk and look for wildlife at the same time. Be safe – stop and then look!

What is up on the roof?

Use binoculars to look up at the roof. Can you see herring gulls and their **nests** there? When the eggs **hatch**, parent gulls feed the chicks scraps of food from rubbish bins and dumps.

Can you spot a pigeon collecting plastic straws or other waste? Pigeons often use these things to make nests. They live off scraps of food that they find in the street.

What grows on the street?

Can you see leaves on the street? They come from trees that grow here. People create areas of soil that trees can grow in among the hard concrete and asphalt streets.

Look at a tree trunk. The **bark** around a tree protects the living plant inside. A plane tree's bark flakes off so the trunk does not get clogged up with **pollution** and dirt.

9

What lives in parks?

Look for clues about what lives in parks. Can you see any animals or insects moving in the trees or gardens?

Squirrels run up and down trees to look for food and save it to eat in winter. Their big front teeth help them to break open nutshells to eat the seeds inside.

11

What lives on walls?

Young ivy plants have floppy **stems**, but can climb up walls. Look for the small **roots** that grow out of the ivy stem. These grow into the wall and hold the plant up.

roots

Look closely at the ivy leaves and flowers. Lots of insects feed on the **nectar** inside the ivy's pale flowers. Spiders spin webs to catch the insects, so they can eat them.

Is the pavement empty?

Is there a silvery trail on the pavement? A snail or a slug is nearby. Snails and slugs make trails of slimy **mucus** that help them glide across the ground to look for food.

Can you see ants carrying tiny bits of food across the pavement? Some ants collect food to take back to their **nests**. They share it with the other ants in their groups.

What lives in the bushes?

Use a magnifying glass to spot insects in the bushes. Insect mouths are shaped to help them eat. Can you see a butterfly's curly **proboscis** sucking **nectar** juice from flowers?

Look for ladybirds with their red and black spots. A ladybird has a hard mouth for crunching tiny insects. Its bright colours warn birds it will taste bad if they eat it.

What animals come out at night?

Look for clues about animals that come out at night. Which animal digs holes like this?

Foxes dig holes called **dens** under sheds or bushes. They have their babies in dens. Foxes eat scraps of meat and other waste food that they find on the street or in rubbish bins.

How can I protect city animals?

Protect city wildlife by putting litter in the bin. Litter can harm animals. They can choke on plastic bags or get trapped inside empty jars.

Use a nature spotter's guide to name wildlife in your neighbourhood. To see more creatures, leave wild areas in the garden where small animals can **shelter**.

Exploring nature

These things will help you explore a city on a nature walk.

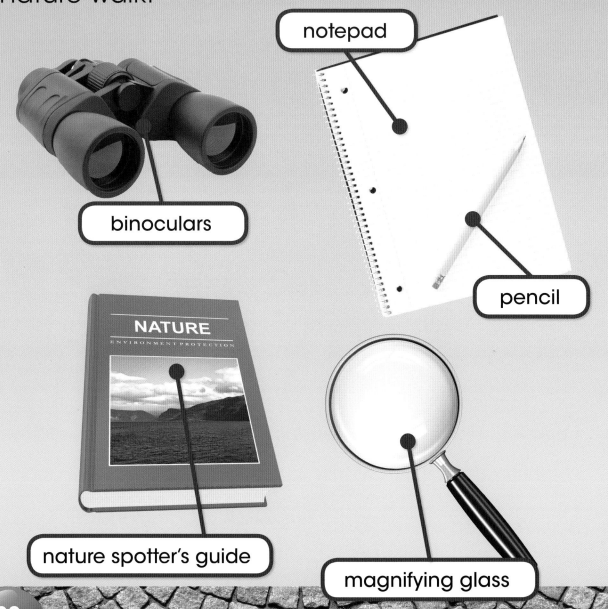

notepad

binoculars

pencil

NATURE
ENVIRONMENT PROTECTION

nature spotter's guide

magnifying glass

Glossary

bark tough layer around a tree trunk

den hole that foxes dig to have their babies in

hatch to come out of an egg

mucus slimy substance animals can make

nectar sweet juice in the centre of a flower

nest place where an animal has its babies

pollution when air, water, or land is damaged or spoiled

proboscis long tube-shaped insect mouth that curls up when not in use

root part of a plant that usually grows underground

shelter to find somewhere safe to live

stem part of a plant that holds up the leaves and flowers

Find out more

Books

In the Garden (Nature Walks),
Clare Collinson
(Franklin Watts, 2010)

Parks and Gardens (Nature
Trails), Anita Ganeri
(Raintree, 2011)

Websites

www.bbc.co.uk/nature/habitats/Urban_ecosystem
Visit this website for facts, videos, and pictures of city wildlife.
You can also download spotters' guides to help you identify
wildlife in the city.

Index

ants 15

butterflies 16

foxes 19

herring gulls 6

insects 13, 15, 16, 17, 10

ivy 12, 13

ladybirds 17

leaves 8, 13

litter 20

pigeons 7

plane trees 9

slugs 14

snails 14

spiders 13

squirrels 11

trees 8, 9, 10, 11